Soccer

Karen Durrie

AV² WORLD LANGUAGES

WORLD LANGUAGES

Go to **openlightbox.com**, and enter the book's unique code.

BOOK CODE

AVU63947

Easily move through highly visual pages.

Toggle between your **14 books** in **14 languages**.

This title is part of our AV2 World Languages digital subscription.

Published by Lightbox Learning Inc.
276 5th Avenue, Suite 704 #917
New York, NY 10001
Website: www.openlightbox.com

Copyright ©2023 Lightbox Learning Inc.

Library of Congress Control Number: 2021952237

ISBN 978-1-7911-4569-9 (hardcover)
ISBN 978-1-7911-4570-5 (multi-user eBook)

Printed in Guangzhou, China
1 2 3 4 5 6 7 8 9 0 26 25 24 23 22

022022
102321

Project Coordinator: John Willis
Designer: Ana María Vidal

The publisher acknowledges Alamy, Getty Images, iStock, and Shutterstock as its primary image suppliers for this title.

2 Access all of the AV2 World Languages titles with our digital subscription.

1-Year World Languages Subscription ISBN
978-1-4896-8345-8

Sign up for a **FREE SUBSCRIPTION**
openlightbox.com/trial

Soccer

Contents

I love soccer. I am going to play soccer today.

4

**Soccer is played
all over the world.** 5

I get dressed for soccer.
I put on my red jersey.
It has a number on its back.

6

Like a
★ Pro

Players on a team wear the same color.

7

I put on my cleats.
They have spikes.
Spikes help me
grip the ground.

8

Like a Pro

Soccer cleats help players control the ball.

I wear shin guards on my legs. I put long socks over them.

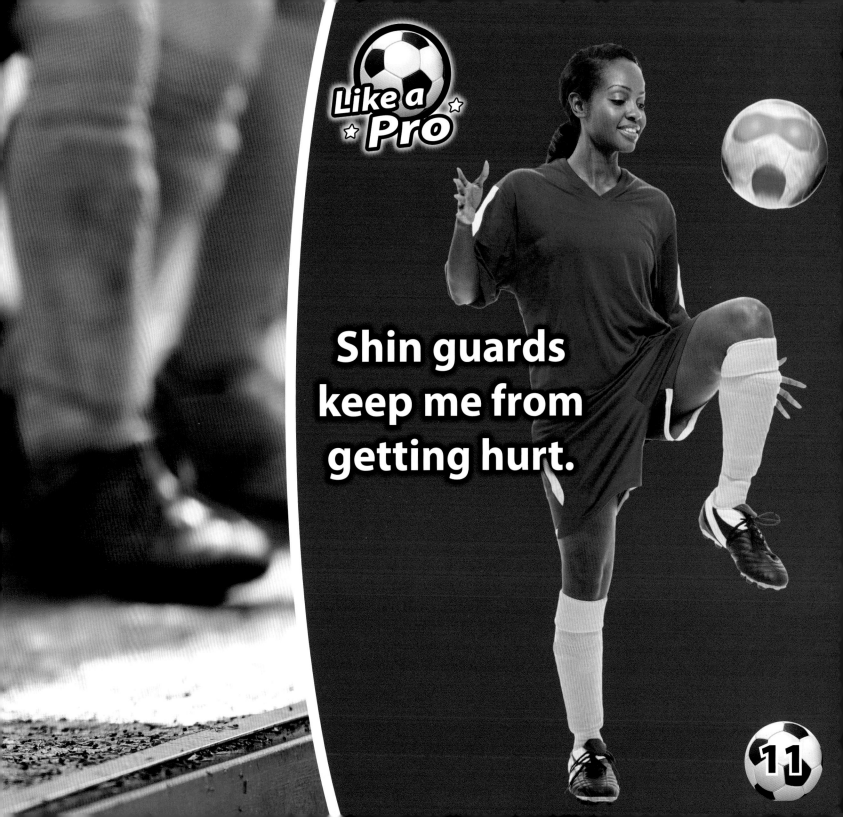

Shin guards keep me from getting hurt.

Like a Pro

11

I have a soccer ball.
It is black and white.
It rolls fast.

Like a Pro

100 million soccer balls are made each year.

13

I meet my friends
to play soccer.
We are a team.

14

Like a Pro

We run and stretch before the game.

15

I am a forward on my team. I do a lot of running. My legs get tired.

Like a Pro

Adult players
can run six miles
in one game.

17

The teams pass, kick, and chase the ball. I score a goal. We win the game.

Like a Pro

One player scores, but teamwork wins a game.

19

I love soccer.

20

SOCCER FACTS

This page provides more detail about the interesting facts found in the book. Simply look at the corresponding page number to match the fact.

Pages 4–5

Getting Ready Soccer is the world's most popular team sport. It can be played almost anywhere. All you need is a level patch of ground, a ball, and two teams. The World Cup is the biggest tournament in professional soccer. Teams from 32 nations play in the World Cup.

Pages 6–7

What I Wear Wearing the same color jersey helps players to quickly identify who is on their team during the fast action on the field. If two teams show up to play a game wearing the same color jerseys, one team will wear shirts called pinnies over their team shirts so players can tell the difference between teams.

Pages 8–9

What I Need Soccer cleats have hard nubs on the bottom that help a player dig into ground that may have bare dirt or slippery spots. Cleats make it easier to run quickly, stop short, and change directions. Indoor soccer players do not wear cleats. Indoor soccer shoes have flat rubber soles to grip artificial turf.

Pages 10–11

More Soccer Gear Playing soccer involves being around lots of flying feet, all running and kicking to get the ball. Many players will be accidentally kicked in the shins during a game. Wearing shin guards helps protect bony shins from injury.

What I Use Soccer balls are usually made of leather and come in three different official sizes, for players of different ages. Soccer balls often have a pattern of hexagons stitched or stamped into the surface. Soccer balls come in many colors and designs. Every four years, a new World Cup soccer ball is designed for that special event.

My Team Cold muscles are stiff, and sudden twisting and turning of them can cause injury. Warming and stretching muscles before playing soccer can reduce the risk of injury. Warm muscles also produce more energy faster. This helps a player run faster and perform with more accuracy and skill.

Playing the Game In youth soccer, there are usually two teams of seven players, including the goalie, on the field. Other players sit on the sidelines to watch and cheer. They wait for the coach to tell them when it is their turn on the field. Players have different jobs to do on the field.

Winning the Game It is exciting to score goals and win games, but learning new skills and enjoying your sport is also important. In soccer, working together as a team by passing the ball and setting up good shots helps a team be successful. If a soccer game is won, it is the team that wins, not just the players that scored goals.

I Love Soccer Playing a sport involves gear and a special place to play. It also involves preparing the body to work hard. Eating healthy food helps fuel the body to do its best. Eating right makes bones stronger and gives muscles energy. A snack and drink after playing sports helps to replace the energy spent during a game.

KEY WORDS

Research has shown that as much as 65 percent of all written material published in English is made up of 300 words. These 300 words cannot be taught using pictures or learned by sounding them out. They must be recognized by sight. This book contains 46 common sight words to help young readers improve their reading fluency and comprehension. This book also teaches young readers several important content words, such as proper nouns. These words are paired with pictures to aid in learning and improve understanding.

Page	Sight Words First Appearance
4	am, I, play, to
5	a, all, is, like, over, the, world
6	back, for, get, has, it, its, my, number, on, put
7	same
8	have, help, me, they
10	long, them
11	from, keep
12	and, white
13	are, each, made, year
14	we
15	before, run
16	do, of
17	can, in, miles, one
19	but

Page	Content Words First Appearance
4	soccer
5	pro
6	jersey
7	color, players, team
8	cleats, ground, spikes
9	ball
10	legs, shin guards, socks
14	friends, team
15	game
16	forward
18	goal
19	teamwork